Frederick O'Neal

ANNA LUCASTA

BY J. P. MILLER

ILLUSTRATED BY
AMANDA QUARTEY

A Division of
Carson Dellosa Education

ROURKE'S
SCHOOL to HOME
CONNECTIONS
BEFORE AND DURING READING ACTIVITIES

Before Reading: *Building Background Knowledge and Vocabulary*

Building background knowledge can help children process new information and build upon what they already know. Before reading a book, it is important to tap into what children already know about the topic. This will help them develop their vocabulary and increase their reading comprehension.

Questions and Activities to Build Background Knowledge:

1. Look at the front cover of the book and read the title. What do you think this book will be about?
2. What do you already know about this topic?
3. Take a book walk and skim the pages. Look at the table of contents, photographs, captions, and bold words. Did these text features give you any information or predictions about what you will read in this book?

Vocabulary: *Vocabulary Is Key to Reading Comprehension*

Use the following directions to prompt a conversation about each word.

- Read the vocabulary words.
- What comes to mind when you see each word?
- What do you think each word means?

> **Vocabulary Words:**
> - audience
> - auditions
> - cast
> - drama
> - equity
> - productions
> - stike
> - theater

During Reading: *Reading for Meaning and Understanding*

To achieve deep comprehension of a book, children are encouraged to use close reading strategies. During reading, it is important to have children stop and make connections. These connections result in deeper analysis and understanding of a book.

 Close Reading a Text

During reading, have children stop and talk about the following:

- Any confusing parts
- Any unknown words
- Text to text, text to self, text to world connections
- The main idea in each chapter or heading

Encourage children to use context clues to determine the meaning of any unknown words. These strategies will help children learn to analyze the text more thoroughly as they read.

When you are finished reading this book, turn to the next-to-last page for **Text-Dependent Questions** and an **Extension Activity**.

TABLE OF CONTENTS

TAKING THE STAGE

Do you work well with others? Do you like being in front of your class? Is it easy for you to remember things?

Frederick O'Neal loved being in front of people and performing as an actor. He was a leader in **theater**.

A long line of people waited on 135th Street in Harlem, New York. They were there for the opening night of the stage play *Anna Lucasta*. It was about to start in the basement of the Schomburg Library.

The Harlem Library Little Theatre

For the first five years, the American Negro Theatre was housed in the basement of the Schomburg Library and was known as the Harlem Library Little Theatre. In 1945, it moved to 126th Street and was renamed the American Negro Theatre Playhouse.

The **cast** was ready. Frederick had learned his lines. The stage was set. All he needed was for the curtain to go up.

Frederick stepped onstage like he owned it. Eyes followed his every move. The **audience** loved him. *Anna Lucasta* was a hit. The stage play eventually moved from Harlem to Broadway.

CENTER STAGE

The family sat around the radio. Squeaking doors and scary voices creeped across the living room. It was radio theater. Young Frederick loved the **drama**. He wanted to be an actor.

Frederick created his own stories. He made his own props. He imitated the actors and created his own place at center stage. Sometimes he made people pay one penny to see his **productions**.

Life changed for Frederick. First, his father died. Then, his family moved from Brooksville, Mississippi, to St. Louis, Missouri.

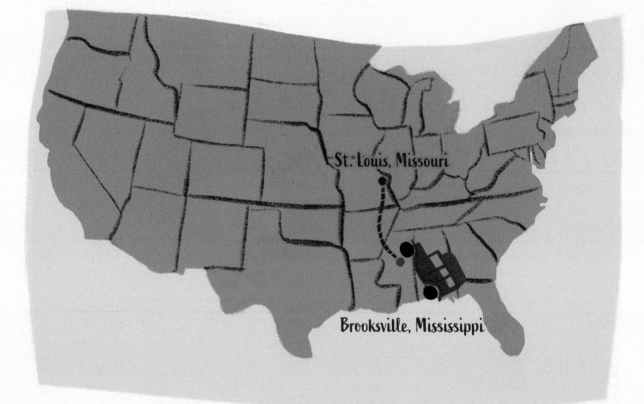

St. Louis, Missouri

Brooksville, Mississippi

Frederick soon found people in St. Louis who loved theater just as much as he did. He performed with them in theaters. It was his first time on a real stage.

A new thing was happening in America. Families no longer sat around the radio for entertainment. They sat around television sets. Acting became even more popular.

Movies were being filmed...

...television shows created...

...stage plays produced.

Most of the actors were white. Black people went to **auditions** but were told there were no parts for them.

Frederick wanted the Black actors of St. Louis to be treated fairly. He helped create the Aldridge Players theater group.

AUDITIONS

The Aldridge Players
The Aldridge Players was a Black theater group. The group was named after Ira Aldridge, who was the first Black actor to play Othello in Shakespeare's play *Othello*.

SOLILOQUY NIG

OPEN

ENT

The Harlem Renaissance was in full swing in the 1930s. Harlem was the place to be for Black literature, music, theater, and art. Black creatives were doing well there.

Frederick O'Neal followed his famous friend, Zora Neale Hurston, to Harlem. She was a leader in the Harlem Renaissance. He took his father's advice with him: To be good at something, do the work.

Zora Neale Hurston

Zora Neale Hurston was a famous writer and filmmaker. She wrote over 50 short stories, plays, and essays. She was best known for her novel *Their Eyes Were Watching God.*

Frederick wanted to be a great actor. He wanted others to be great, too. With friend Abram Hill, he started the American Negro Theatre. Frederick enjoyed teaching people how to act. Sidney Poitier, Harry Belafonte, and Ruby Dee were all students of his who went on to be movie stars.

Frederick was the voice for Black actors. For eighteen years, he was president of the Associated Actors and Artistes of America. For part of that time, he was also President of the Actors' **Equity** Association. Frederick negotiated pay raises for actors in the 1960s. This helped end an actors' **strike**.

Frederick worked in theater, television, and movies for 44 years. He made things better for Black actors in America. He also helped start the British Negro Theatre to make things better for Black actors in London, England. He is best known for his roles in the stage play *Anna Lucasta* and television show *Car 54, Where Are You?*

Frederick was inducted into the Black Filmmakers Hall of Fame in 1975. In 1979, the NAACP named him "Man of the Year." Frederick O'Neal died in New York, New York, in 1992 at the age of 86.

"The theater requires total commitment and dedication, and even then, a person may not be successful.

—Frederick O'Neal

TIME LINE

1905   Frederick O'Neal is born on August 27th in Brooksville, MS.

1919   Frederick's father dies and the family moves to
St. Louis, MO.

1927   Frederick starts the Black theater group the Aldridge Players.

1936   Frederick moves to New York. He debuts the same year with
the Civic Repertory Theatre.

1940   Frederick cofounds the American Negro Theatre with writer,
Abram Hill.

1944   Frederick debuts on Broadway in the hit stage play
Anna Lucasta.

1948   Frederick helps found the British Negro Theater in London.

1963-64 Frederick portrays Officer Wallace on the hit television
show *Car 54, Where Are You?*

1964-73 Frederick becomes the president of the Actors' Equity
Association. He was the first Black person to do so.

1970-88 Frederick is elected president of the Associated Actors and
Artistes of America. He serves in the position for 18 years.

1975   Frederick is inducted into the Black Filmmakers Hall of Fame.

1979   The NAACP names Frederick O'Neal "Man of the Year."

1992   Frederick O'Neal dies on August 25th at age 86.

GLOSSARY

audience (AW-dee-uhns): the people who watch or listen to a performance, such as a play

auditions (aw-DISH-uhns): a short performance by someone, such as an actor, to see whether they are suitable for a part in a performance, such as a play or movie

cast (kast): the actors in a play, movie, or television program

drama (DRAH-muh): the subject or practice of acting

equity (EK-wi-tee): equal treatment for everyone in a situation

productions (pruh-DUHK-shuhns): any forms of entertainment that are presented to others

strike (strike): a situation in which workers refuse to work until their demands are met

theater (THEE-uh-tur): the work of writing, producing, or acting in plays

INDEX

TEXT-DEPENDENT QUESTIONS

1. What is an actors' strike?

2. What organizations did Frederick O'Neal help start?

3. Where was the play *Anna Lucasta* performed?

4. Name a few of Frederick O'Neal's students who became famous actors.

5. What are some of the ways Frederick O'Neal changed things for Black actors?

EXTENSION ACTIVITY

How well can you act? Gather your friends and/or family around to find out! Divide into two teams. Take turns being the actor. The actor will choose the name of a movie, TV show, or play to act out for their team. Set a timer for two minutes. If your team guesses what you're acting out correctly, your team gets a point. Oh...and did I say without talking? Keep going until everyone has a chance to be the actor. Have fun!

ABOUT THE AUTHOR

J.P. Miller Growing up, J.P. Miller loved reading stories that she could become immersed in. As a writer, she enjoys doing the same for her readers. Through the gift of storytelling, she is able to bring little- and well-known people and events in African American history to life for young readers. She hopes that her stories will augment the classroom experience and inspire her readers. J.P. lives in metro Atlanta and is the author of the *Careers in the US Military* and *Black Stories Matter* series. J.P. is the winner of the 2021 Black Authors Matter Award sponsored by the National Black Book Festival.

ABOUT THE ILLUSTRATOR

Amanda Quartey Amanda lives in the UK and was born and bred in London. She has always loved to draw and has been doing so ever since she can remember. At the age of 14, she moved to Ghana and studied art in school. She later returned to the UK to study graphic design. Her artistic path deviated slightly when she studied Classics at her university. Over the years, in a bid to return to her artistic roots, Amanda has built a professional illustration portfolio and is now loving every bit of her illustration career.

www.rourkeeducationalmedia.com

Quote source: Rule, Sheila. "Black Actor's Self-Determined Performance," St. Louis Post-Dispatch (St. Louis, MO), September 12, 1972: https://www.newspapers.com/image/139436266/

Edited by: Hailey Scragg
Illustrations by: Amanda Quartey
Cover and interior layout by: J.J. Giddings

Library of Congress PCN Data

Frederick O'Neal / J.P. Miller
(Leaders Like Us)
ISBN 978-1-73165-179-2 (hard cover)
ISBN 978-1-73165-224-9 (soft cover)
ISBN 978-1-73165-194-5 (e-Book)
ISBN 978-1-73165-209-6 (ePub)
Library of Congress Control Number: 2021944520

Rourke Educational Media
Printed in the United States of America
01-3402111937